Teacher, Teacher!
Did you know...

by

Jo Anne Spiceland

Teacher, Teacher!
Did you know...

Jo Anne Spiceland

McClanahan
Publishing House

Copyright ©1995 by Jo Anne Spiceland

ISBN 0-913383-39-2

All rights reserved.

No part of this book may be copied
or reproduced without permission from
the publisher, except by a reviewer who may quote brief
passages in a review.

*Cover design and book layout by James Asher Graphics.
Title art by Max Krone*

Manufactured in the United States of America.

All book order correspondence should be addressed to:

Jo Anne Spiceland
7206 Benton Road
Paducah, KY 42003
502-898-2830

McClanahan
Publishing House

*Give a little love to a child,
and you get a great deal back.*

*Dedicated to
Rodney Herrold
and
Larry Harper*

Teacher, Teacher! Did you know...

The information learned from "kids" in school makes teaching a lot of fun.

Everything in this book was learned from kindergarten or second grade students. It's great that they share so much information with you. It often makes your days so nice—it gives you a time to laugh. And it's wonderful that children trust their teachers and ask them so many questions!

Over the years a "newspaper" was sent to the parents each month and lots of their humorous things were shared with them. The parents enjoyed seeing the funny things too, and they would often say, "I <u>know</u> my child said that!"

All things written here were said by students, but, of course, this is not <u>all</u> they said! There is no way you could get things written down every day—not enough time! And some things they tell you, you couldn't share with parents!

Teaching is a difficult job. With a room full of children whom you are trying to teach and direct in the proper ways, the day can be a long day! Each child is special and many learn in different ways and teachers must plan for each child and try to make sure all students learn to their own ability. But children can be fun! Listening to all the things they tell you will often make your day hilarious.

Over the years, I have written down many of the things my students have told me. Reading and discussing them with friends makes teaching more fun. So, even though teaching requires lots of work, learning about all your students and accepting them as part of your own family for the rest of their lives makes teaching school fun and a loving job.

The following "tales" are things the children have told me. Many times a year I have sent home letters to their parents and revealed to them some of the "funnies" their children had told me at school. All of this information is from children ages five to seven. And when they come in and start saying, "Teacher, Teacher, did you know. . . ." you'll remember that teaching school is GREAT.

Teacher, Teacher, did you know
All I tell you is <u>really</u> so?
I know lots of funny stuff
But I work and work quite enough!
Everywhere I go I see—
Lots of things that are new to me.
And going to school is lots of fun
But I can't get everything done.
My favorite thing is playing outside
Then we can run and jump and hide!
Inside playing is funny, too,
But, Teacher, I want to tell you—
Too much working, I do a lot
But school is still my favorite spot.
I am playing and working and learning, too!
It's fun to be at school with you.

Teacher, Teacher! Did you know...

Kids are cute
Kids aren't bad
Kids are the funniest
Things I've had!

Kids are great
Kids work hard.
Kids are good players
In school yards.

Kids are sweetest
Things I've met.
Do I love them?
Yes! You bet!!!

Remember kids
Day and night?
Yes, we all do—
That is right!

Kids are special
To teachers—All
Teaching school
You have a ball!

In the school
Teaching is fun.
Do we love them?
Yes!!! Every one!

Jo Anne Spiceland

Quotes from the Kids

"Teacher, if you'd practice, you could be a cheerleader."

"Last year I thought being a teacher was an easy job. But now that I'm in the second grade, I realize that it takes a lot of hard work just getting to BE a teacher."

"My dad won't let me be a cheerleader—
he says their dresses are too short."

Student: "I think she has sexy legs."
Teacher: "What are sexy legs?"
Student: "Legs that are pretty and don't have bruises on them."

Teacher, Teacher! Did you know...

After getting a math paper back and
seeing a missed problem:
> "I know this problem is right—
> I've got all those combinations
> right here in my head."

Can we make up a story just like we're telling the truth?"

> "Teacher, I have an upset tooth."

"I think I'm allergic to strep throat."

> "My daddy just has hair
> on the sides of his head
> and his legs."

I've been out of school
because I had <u>antibodies</u>."

> "I found some money in our car—in the glove
> <u>department</u>." (compartment)

> "Granddaddy gives me a hug
> and I hug him around his belly."

Jo Anne Spiceland

"Daddy says we're going to church just as soon as Mother loses enough weight so she can get her some clothes."

Teacher, Teacher! Did you know...

"I went to Africa last summer and got on a hippo and it went into the water and I drowned."

"I don't feel well—my liver hurts."

"I kissed Tammy and she sure had bad breath."

"Teacher, someone at church sang a song that said, 'Jesus is in your heart and that's all that's in your heart.' But that's not right 'cause Winnie the Pooh is in mine."

After telling the children about Queen Isabella, Christopher Columbus, his ships, etc., a voice came from the rear of the class,
    "Teacher, was that World War I or World War II?"

"Last night my throat was stuck."

"I felt bad last night but I feel badder today."

"This summer I had infant tiger
    and I had to put medicine on it."

Jo Anne Spiceland

"Teacher! Look! There are
two flies riding piggyback
on our window!"

    Looking at wood chips under the swings:
        "Well, that's enough or more than enough
        chips to play poker."

    "That rabbit looks like a Playboy Bunny."

At listening center:
    "My earmuffs aren't turned on yet."

    "I want to stay in Kindergarten forever!
    But then I'd have to be a midget, wouldn't I?"

    "My grandpa is almost not dead yet."

"I can't read this book, Teacher,
all I can read is Chinese and Russian."

    "My mom is in love with Tom Selleck."

> "I know that word
>   —I can't say it—
>   it's on the tip of my ear."

Teacher, Teacher! Did you know...

"Do you know that my
mother and daddy used
to live with their parents?"

"I think I can read—but only cursive writing."

> "Teacher, I bet it's been a long time since
> you got a heart with 'I Love You' on it."

"I know why I cuss—my mama and my daddy do!"

   "My coat is made out of Hong Kong."

"Have I said my Januarys yet?" (Months of the year)

"My mom works at a funeral home
where they make sick people well."

"I don't aim to ever get married but I may just have to in
order to get a man."

> "My daddy is going to be a semi today."

   "Whee! This is what we call a 'sweatin' day!"

Jo Anne Spiceland

Going over the alphabet: "Teacher, I didn't even know they made all of those letters!"

"I can't believe it
but my mama says
she used to live
with my granddaddy."

"My favorite drink is beer mixed
with just a little bit of Pepsi."

While looking at a deep hole being dug for construction:
"I'd be afraid to dig a hole like that! I'd be afraid
the devil might come out!"

"I can tell time—it's twenty o'clock."

"I am working so hard I think
I'll have a nervous breakdown."

"I think I'll like school by the
time I get into the eighth grade."

"I pulled a muscle out of my leg last night."

Teacher, Teacher! Did you know...

"Next week my mom is going
to the hospital to stay forever!"

"Teacher, can we have the word 'sex' on our spelling test?
I know lots about that."

"My mom is going to have a baby
but I'm not supposed to tell it."

"My mother said not to tell you
why I was absent yesterday, but I think I will.
We went to the circus. She wrote a note and
said I was sick, but I wasn't."

"Teacher, can we start a
Women's Liberation team at recess?"

"I got an eight-dollar bill for Christmas."

Student to student:
"Get that fat off your face! It looks terrible!"

"I think life is very confusing."

Jo Anne Spiceland

"I'd like to be a belly dancer when I grow up."

"I went to the dentist
and I didn't have any cavities at all.
He just filled three holes in my teeth."

"Teacher, do you know why I named my pet 'Kitty'?
Because it's a cat!"

"I'm never going to get married—
I'm just going to live in a cabin."

"Teacher, look! I can really make a good five."
"You've really been practicing at home!"
"No, I practiced at church yesterday."

"Teacher, can I go unsharpen my pencil?"

"Teacher, he said the baddest word—PUKE."

"The more times you get married,
the more kids you can have.
You can have sixty or forty."

"Every time I get married,
I'm going to marry the same man."

"Teacher, I don't want to do this work.
I think I'm just bored."

"I'm never going to get married—
I'm just going to be a ball player."

"My grandmother is named after my mother."

"My dad is half a policeman."

"My mother makes money.
She just gets paper and draws pictures on it."

"Teacher, did you buy these pumpkins?
Boy, you must be a billionaire!"

"My daddy had to fix my hair
and he isn't very good at hair doing."

"Why is the principal so mean?
Every time he sees me running he grabs my arm!"

"We keep finding cow legs
in our yard every morning."

"You'd better let me go to the bathroom
'cause I have to do an emergency."

Jo Anne Spiceland

"I don't have to hold up my fingers
to count anymore—
I have fingers in my head."

Teacher, Teacher! Did you know...

"Teacher, do these kids
 ever get on your nerves?"

Jo Anne Spiceland

"I'd like a cheerleading doll for Christmas."

"Well, Teacher, I screwed up again!"

"When Indian girls get married,
do they just put a white sheet over their head?"

"My daddy wants a baby so my
mama says he can just have it."

"When my dog goes off,
he is always looking for a girl friend."

"Did you know my mama still owes for the Christmas presents?"

"Our snacks today are just like dinner at church.

"If there isn't a Santa Claus,
how come my daddy can talk
to him on the phone?"

Teacher, Teacher! Did you know...

"I think that happened the day before Valentine's Eve."

"I did the splits and I cut my bladder open."

"Are we going out on the mountain at recess?" (hillside)

"Look at me! I can dance just like a maniac!"

"Will we ever play
Dungeons and Dragons
in Kindergarten?"

"Teacher, these kids are getting on my nerves."

"Teacher, I KNOW ten plus ten is not twenty—
my daddy said it isn't."

"My uncle had a baby last night."

"Teacher, I don't know
if you know this or not
 but she says she is going
to sex one of the boys at recess."

"My mother won't buy coffee any more.
She says it's too high. So she just goes to
Grandmother's each day to drink coffee."

Jo Anne Spiceland

"Last night I got hit in my eye
and my eye almost got broke."

"When I get a broken leg, I'm going to
come to school and let everyone sign it."

"Teacher, did you get your hair cut last night?"
"No."
"Well, I guess you just got it bent a different way."

"What is wrong with her?
I think she has contagious again."

Student 1: "What do buckskins come from?"
Student 2: "A man deer."

"Teacher, is Jesus' last name Christ?"

"If Santa isn't real,
is God and Jesus real?"

"It's awfully hard to think when you don't have a thinker."

"Daddy chases my mother all over our house."

Teacher, Teacher! Did you know...

"When I was in preschool, I had
twenty-two hours of recess every day."

        "Teacher, how do you make a capital '5'?"

        "Teacher, this is the best school I've ever been in."
        "How many schools have you been in?"
        "None!"

"Teacher, do you think the boys would notice
if I wore my bikini to school?"

        "My brother had a high fever
        last night and we had to pack
        him in ice cream."

        "Teacher, I can do about all the skating things—
        even the squats."

Boy 1: "I'd like to have babies when I grow up."
Boy 2: "If you did that you'd have to have a sex change."

        "My boyfriend gave me a box of candy for
        Valentine's Day—but he ate some of it first."

"Is four rabbits and four rabbits eight rabbits?"

        "It's eleven more years 'til my birthday."

Jo Anne Spiceland

"Teacher, look at him!
He's going wild today!
I don't believe a Kindergartner
should be wild."

> "My daddy says bad words
> but he won't let me so I just say son-of-a-gun."

"For recreation, my daddy goes to bars."

> "I can tickle the ceiling
> of my mouth with my tongue."

"My colors (crayons) are getting weared out."

> "It ain't nice to get married
> when you're in Kindergarten, is it?"

"I'm not afraid of tornadoes. I told God not to send one and He won't."

Student: "Both of my brothers is in Cub Scouts."
Teacher: "Really? How old are they?"
Student: "One is 19 and the other one is 60."

> Boy: "Teacher, don't girls wear
> see-through dresses so we can see more?"

Teacher, Teacher! Did you know...

"My mom and me just love to kick Daddy out of the house every chance we get. Then we can do what we please."

"I have two brothers— one real and one imaginary."

Student 1: "I wear my down jacket when I go hunting."
Student 2: "What do you hunt?"
Student 1: "Mostly girls."
Student 2: "That's nothing. I hunt everything there is to hunt on this earth except snake lips."

"Teacher, when we all die and go to Heaven, maybe you'll be our Kindergarten teacher again."

Looking at a plus (+) sign on the board:
"Look, Teacher, a church pole."

"Teacher, smell of me.
I smell just like my dad."

"My Valentine man is handicapped."

"My granddaddy is married to my grandmother."

Jo Anne Spiceland

"I'm not drinking much water any more.
I'm trying to save water."

"I hope we get to go back to church
before the preacher forgets my name."

"Teacher, do you know what thunder is?
It's God's angels bowling."

Teacher, Teacher! Did you know...

"When the sun and the
wind crash together,
that makes lightning."

"Teacher, do bugs go to bed at night
when their mama tells them to?"

Student: "I don't like school."
Teacher: "Well, I'm sorry, but
 you'll have to come anyway."
Student: "Even if I'm sick?"
Teacher: "Yes."
Student: "Even if I have hepatitis?"

"Right now, all I have to do at home is rabbit watching. But when our new baby gets here, I'll have to do baby watching."

"When my mom had a baby,
she had to stay in the hospital
for one hundred years."

"My house is so messy
that when I get home
it gives me the creeps!"

Student 1: "Mom got married again last night."
Student 2: "Well, that's nothing. My mom's been
 married five times."

Jo Anne Spiceland

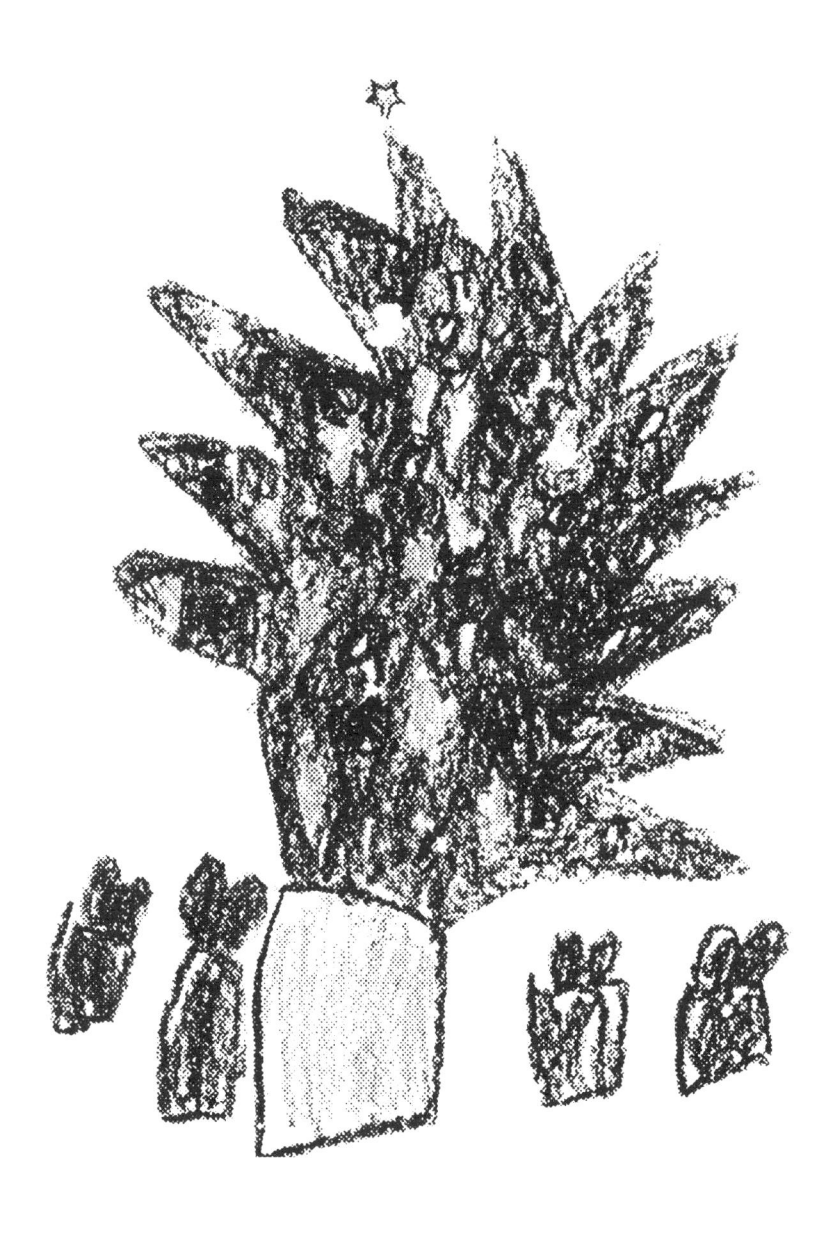

"My mother growled at my daddy last night
when we were putting up the Christmas tree."

Teacher, Teacher! Did you know...

Girl to teacher:
    "He's a bigger pain now
      than he was in Preschool!"

Jo Anne Spiceland

"My daddy doesn't work—
he just plays around."

"My aunt is coming to visit us today
and I haven't seen her in sixteen years."

"I got my feet fingernails polished."

"We had a fire hydrant drill today."

"I think all the Kindergarten work is just ridiculous!"

Girl to girl:
"Hey, you really need to shave your legs!"

"I go to the Salvation Church."

"When our baby comes, if it is a boy,
I'm going to put it in a box and take
it to the Post Office and send it back."

"My daddy doesn't have to get a haircut very often. He's almost bald. And that saves us money."

"My dad is sick. He's down on his back."

Teacher, Teacher! Did you know...

"My grandparents got on a plane
and flew almost to the sun."

"Teacher, I'm in love
but I wouldn't tell anyone
for everything in the whole world."

After a hot recess:
"Teacher, if God is in my heart
I'll bet he is on fire 'cause I'm burning up!"

"We got a brand new car yesterday for fifty dollars."

"You know what's good about making T's?
You can't make them backwards."

"Do people really have butterfingers?"

"I was upset at my stomach this weekend."

"Teacher, my cat has a boyfriend now."

Jo Anne Spiceland

"Teacher, we had to get my cat sewed up
 'cause her boyfriend lived across the street
and he wouldn't stay away."

"Teacher, I made a mistake
and that's the last one
I'm ever going to make
as long as I live."

"My mom said to tell you that YES
is not spelled T-E-S like you told me."

"My dad rode a camel
at the Donkey Ballgame last night."

"You can't get married until you have
chicken pox so you might as well get them
and get it over with."

"Teacher, when you are not at school
do you just sit around and draw pictures?"

Teacher, Teacher! Did you know...

"We have added a junk yard inside our house."

"We are fixing a library at our house
and me and my mom are going to live there
and let Daddy stay in the bedroom."

"My girl friend is fat but I love her anyway."

"I didn't bring my money today. My mom is grouchy about money in the mornings."

"Teacher, when I go to high school,
I will graduate.
Teacher, did you do that?"

"Teacher, I don't like
sitting next to these girls.
I just can't keep from touching them."

"I went to the doctor
and he said I had a throat ache."

"My dog laid baby pups last night."

"I saw Easter Bunny tracks
beside my house yesterday."

Teacher, Teacher! Did you know...

"My mama's daddy died one time."

"Teacher, she says I'm disgusting today!"

"My emotions are just all shook up today."

"My dad didn't want his dog
to have any more puppies
so he took her to the vet
and had her tail cut off."

"Teacher, did you know my daddy is a boy?"

"My mom is going to look for a job today
but she wants one where she doesn't have to work."

"We're going to Daytona Beach
for a vacation and while we're there,
we'll probably go to Florida."

"I have some bad news.
I think we may have to pay our taxes."

"My mom named me Tina
after I told her what a 'T' said."

Jo Anne Spiceland

"We have a new calf—
the mama cow just popped it out."

"Teacher, my tonsils are loose!"

"Look at my watch—
it's water resistance."

"My dog's girl friend had babies
'caused my dog sexed her."

"You'd better say your prayers now 'cause you'll have to work all day in the first grade!"

"We got some eggs and laid them in a cup
for six years and then they hatched."

"My daddy quit his job
'cause he only got paid seven dollars a week."

"My dad borrowed my birthday money
to get Mom a Mother's Day present."

Teacher, Teacher! Did you know...

"When I grow up, I'm going to live close to a MacDonald's or a park—I don't know which."

"We went fishing the day after yesterday."

"I don't have snack money this week— our new TV cost too much money."

"My brother's tonsils are almost glued together."

"If you go to Wendy's you can get a Big Mac."

Teacher: "Do you know what kind of tree this acorn came from?"
Student: "Yes, and ache tree!"

"My coat has a name—it's a vest."

"My dog found a shot deer in the woods and we tried to find a deer doctor but we couldn't."

"My mom has been using bad manners."

Jo Anne Spiceland

"I can tell a boy cat from a girl cat
by looking at their faces."

Teacher, Teacher! Did you know...

"If Christmas doesn't come soon,
 I'm going to have a nervous breakdown!"

Jo Anne Spiceland

"I had stitches in my head
and you can still feel the crack."

"We're going out to eat tonight
because we don't have any food at home."

"My dad doesn't like to go to church
'cause you have to shut your eyes."

"My mother had kittens today."

"My mom is going to be pregnant
in eight more months."

"Teacher, I just can't do this! I haven't exercised in years!"

Student 1: "I used to live in my mother's belly!"
Student 2: "It isn't her belly—it's her uterus!"

Teacher, Teacher! Did you know...

"I'll bet when school ends Friday
        we'll all be saying 'Thank the Lord!' "

    "I saw a cow yesterday
    that was fatter than my mom!"

"Teacher, help me draw my name."

        "My boy friend is a carpenter
        and he can paste really good."

Teacher, trying to elicit the word FROST:
    "And what was it that happened all over
    our yards last night?"
Student: "Revival!"

"Last night I forgot to say my prayers and I saw a witch outside my window. Then I said my prayers and an angel flew into my room."

      "If you are 65, it's time you tired."

"I have a new ring
and it's just like a married ring."

    "Halloween is a time when your tongue
    has a good time tasting all the treats you get."

Jo Anne Spiceland

After seeing an opera:
"Teacher, I can't even yell THAT loud."

"Some people say that bank people
know more than teachers."

"Know who won the ballgame last night—
the blue-shirted ones."

"My sister has had all kinds of boy friends
but she has finally found one that will marry her."

Student 1: "Look! I'm done!"
Student 2: "Well, look at me—I'm <u>doner</u>."

"All the penguins live together at the South pole
and I'll bet they have a BIG house!"

"If you got married
you may have to kiss your husband."

"My uncle has a beard just like a ground hog."

"My mother is going to have to work the rest of her life—
'til she's 82."

Teacher, Teacher! Did you know...

"Teacher, I wish you could see my daddy in his underwear—he's fat. I mean REALLY fat."

"My mom had a baby last night. Nobody knows it yet and we're keeping it a secret from Daddy."

"We've got just a plum common dog at home."

Jo Anne Spiceland

Student: "We got robbed last night and I got a gun and shot him."
Teacher: "Really? Do you know who he was?"
Student: "No, I forgot to get his autograph."

"Teacher, did your mother divorce you?"

"I acted real sick at the store last night and my mom bought me a toy."

"My granny is coming to visit us and she just spoils us rotten!"

"I had cow meat for lunch today."

"If the preacher calls our house my dad says he'll take care of him!"

"My brother is six years old and is now in the sixth grade. Since I am five, why can't I go to the fifth grade?"

After an "accident" at recess:
Teacher: "Are you feeling better?"
Student: "Yes, but just a little bit of my memory is gone."

Teacher, Teacher! Did you know...

"I'm going to be a nurse when I grow up and burp babies."

"Teacher, come here and help me make an upside down 'M'."

"I learn songs while I am sleeping at night."

"I want a pet but I know I'd pester it to death if I had one."

"My dad is 31 and my mom is 30. Dad's old but Mama isn't."

"My dad is going to be the Chili Man at the Fall Festival."

"Teacher, something has to be done about these wild kids!"

"Will you give me a ticket for being good today?"

"Teacher, listen, I can speak English."

"My mom has some earrings that cost eight hundred thousand dollars."

Jo Anne Spiceland

"Teacher, do you have any boy dresses
at the Dress Up Center?"

Student at recess went up and started rubbing the teacher's back.
Teacher: "Oh, that feels good!"
Student: "Well, I didn't come to school to rub your back. I came to learn ABC's."

"At recess, I'm going to work out making me a friend."

"I've got a new brand dress on today."

"About every four years
we have to go to the grocery."

"We can't go to Granny's house
'cause it takes all the money we have to buy gas."

"My mom is buying all her
Christmas presents with a MasterCard."

"Teacher, if they don't let me play with
them at recess, I'm going to run off to Ohio."

Teacher, Teacher! Did you know...

Teacher: "Who celebrated the first Thanksgiving?"
Student: "God."
Teacher: "Why did the Pilgrims come to this country?"
Student: "To eat turkey."

"My dad built our house
one hundred years ago today."

Jo Anne Spiceland

On George Washington's birthday, we had a cherry pie. "Teacher, do you think these cherries came from the tree he chopped down?"

"Teacher, I'm going to have to skin my crayons."

"My shoe ate my sock."

"I ate ten gallons of pizza last night."

"Teacher, what I did to him was an accident—on purpose."

Child has been out sick:
Teacher: "And how are you feeling today?"
Student: "Just spectacular!"

"Teacher, just wait 'til you see the fancy panties I wore to school today!"

"Teacher, I won't be coming to school any more 'cause I'm pregnant."

Teacher, Teacher! Did you know...

"I found ten thousand bucks
and my daddy let me keep it all."

"Tomorrow we're going to a motel
and Daddy's going to shoot at it."

"My dad weighs nineteen hundred pounds."

"My grandmother is twenty-five years old."

"I love corn. It has so much calcium in it."

"I've had an X-ray. They just X-rayed the gross parts of me but I won't tell you where."

"My feet are hurting 'cause they are getting so tall."

"Teacher, will you stay in the bathroom
while my daddy brings my pet?"
"Well, I don't know. Why?"
" 'Cause I'm afraid you might
fall in love with my daddy!"

"As quick as I grow up
I'm going to find someone to marry."

"My mom was a teenager before she married."

Jo Anne Spiceland

"My dad climbed on the roof and slid down the chimney. We had a fire going and boy! was he surprised!"

"My dog had puppies—
nearly a million. And boy,
did we have a time
giving them all away!"

"Don't tell anyone but my aunt
is married to my uncle."

"A baby came out of my
mommy's stomach
and I got to see it."

"My grandmother is dead
but I think she once saw a dinosaur."

Student 1: "My dad is thirteen years old."
Student 2: "He couldn't be thirteen! He'd be dead!"

"Teacher, I'm going to practice when I get home."
"What are you going to practice?"
"Nothing, just practice."

Teacher, Teacher! Did you know...

"I've got a whole bathing suit for summer."

"I can make a half way duck call."

"Why do we celebrate Easter?"
" 'Cause we need new clothes."

"Teacher, I need a new tooth report card."

"Teacher, write me a note about how much money I owe. I keep forgetting it 'cause I've got to keep a phone number in my mind."

"Well, I'd better put my mouth to sleep today."

"I want to go tell my girl friend that she'll like my dad 'cause he is so handsome."

"We're going on a vacation on February 30."

"I'm going to give you a shot and it will hurt so just sit there and pray to God."

"My dad's a little bit naked on the top of his head."

Jo Anne Spiceland

"I don't think I would come to my church
if I were you, Teacher. It's just too hard to find."

"I got hit in the head with a golf ball
and part of my brain just fell out."

"My dog sleeps in the closet where the mouses is."

"Teacher, is God bigger than my dad?"

"I saw a picture of Jesus
and I know that Jesus is a girl."

"I'll bring a hamster to school tomorrow
if we can go to California tonight and get one."

"My next door neighbor had puppies last night."

"Teacher, is tomorrow the next day?"

"My father's daddy's parents are going to pick me up tomorrow. I have to go to the dentist and get my tonsils out."

Teacher, Teacher! Did you know...

"My boy friend is a real love bird!"

"We made pear honey at home last night. We mashed up some pears and put some stuff the bees made in it."

"We've got a virus in our house somewhere but we can't find it."

(Parent, late picking up child)
"Well, Mom is probably at a Yard Sale and she just forgot the time."

Jo Anne Spiceland

"My dad said he used to be
two years old but I don't believe it."

"My daddy brings home fifteen dollars every day.
It ain't no money—it's just a check."

"Teacher, I'm glad I have cat eyes
then I can tell you when any one
does something wrong."

"My mother told me not to drink milk today.
She said if I did and I went outside it would
freeze inside me."

"I'm pretending I'm forty-eight
and having a baby."

Teacher: "And why did the Pilgrims
come to the United States?"
Student: "To get away from God."

Student at Dress UP Center:
"Wait! I can't have my baby
'til I get my pajamas on!"

Girl: "Teacher, don't boys have sex symbols?"

Teacher, Teacher! Did you know...

"Teacher, did you know
      it takes a long time to have a
      baby and you have to push real hard?"

Boy to Girl:
    "You'd better watch out!
    I may be the Kissing Bandit soon.

        "Teacher, will you just look at this garb
        my mother made me wear to school?"

          "I'm half a millionaire—
          I'm almost rich—
          I have one hundred dollars."

"Guess what? We have lots of money.
My dad gave my mom forty dollars last night."

        "I'm drinking lots of milk
        so I can wear skirts to school."

The first day of school:
    "Well, our vacation is plumb over!"

    "We had recess at home last night."

        "My friend and I killed a rattlesnake
        and a cobra and a python this summer."

Jo Anne Spiceland

"My mother is going to have a baby.
        I think it will be either a boy or a girl."

"My mama used to work for gas grills."

    "Teacher, I'm wilder than a March hare today!"

"When you get married,
you have to have a baby
even if you don't want to."

Teacher, Teacher! Did you know...

"Teacher, doesn't everyone have step sisters?"

"I was hatched from an egg."

"My mom is eighty-eight years old."

"My dog may never have puppies.
She doesn't like her new husband."

"My dad drinks beer but he
doesn't want anybody to know it."

"My mom's all done having babies."

"Teacher, do you think the boys would notice
if I wore my see-through top to school?"

"Teacher, can I show my new panties
to everyone at Circle Time?"

Student 1: "My grandmother lives in Heaven."
Student 2: "What did she go for?"

"My granny says she is going to disown me
because I voted for George Bush."

Jo Anne Spiceland

"I know all about dinosaurs
 but I am NOT going to be a scientist!"

      "Teacher, did you know
      my daddy used to be a teenager?"

"Teacher, those kids are talking about something they know absolutely nothing about."

      "Our preacher got chased by a bull."

    "I'm never going to date when I grow up—
    I'm just going to college."

"I hate to think about marriage
—whew!—all that kissing!"

        "You can eat faster than me
        'cause you have a bigger mouth."

"Teacher, you can't start being Indian-blooded, can you?"

Teacher, Teacher! Did you know...

    "I'm never going to get married!
    I'm never going to have kids!
    I love to sleep by myself."

Going over alphabet:
    "I didn't know they even
    made some of those letters!"

    "My other teacher
    had a desk just like yours,
    but it wasn't messy."

"If I had a dinosaur,
I think I could impress my whole neighborhood."

    "I just love to learn about dinosaurs
    and all the people who lived back then."

    "My mother can eat faster than a pig."

"Teacher, I had a heart attack at recess."

    "The only food we have
    in our house is five potatoes."

    "I don't know what that letter is
    but I know it's in the alphabet."

Jo Anne Spiceland

Teacher, Teacher! Did you know...

"Teacher, do people go to dog's heaven?"

"My daddy killed a bear—
the kind that stands on its own behind feet."

"Our new house cost
one thousand two hundred dollars.
We were lucky."

"I have a half-way cousin
who just moved to our town."

"I go to the Ledbetter Elementary Church."

"We went out to eat at Service Merchandise last night."

"My daddy won't buy
Mom candy for Valentine's Day—
she's too fat already."

"That kid looks like a farmer—
he has SO much mud on him!"

"Teacher, did you go on a date Saturday night?
I saw you with a man."

Jo Anne Spiceland

"We're going to a dancing class
for women who want to lose weight."

"This room is getting too stuffed with kids!"

"See this old shirt?
I've had it for centuries
since I was four years old."

"Teacher, do you
have any logical reason
for keeping us in today?"

When making Ground Hog puppets:
 "Teacher, my dog is dry!"

"Teacher, I want to tell you something
that happened a couple of yesterdays ago."

"Teacher, I have so many girl friends
I just can't handle them all!"

"I can't do my work
'cause it makes my hands hot."

Teacher, Teacher! Did you know...

"I saw a dead snake and it bit me."

"I want to be a dinosaur boner when I grow up."

Teacher: "And who is president of our country?"
Student: "Johnny Carson!"

"I don't want to be anything when I grow up—
I just want to live with my mom."

"I sure hope I get home in time to see
'The Days of Our Lives'—I love soap operas."

"My grandmother ate dinner
with Abraham Lincoln one time
when she was in Kindergarten."

"My sister has a boyfriend. I like him too.
No wonder they go outside and kiss!"

"When I get to be thirty-five,
I'm going to go scuba diving for treasures.
Then I'll be rich."

Jo Anne Spiceland

Student: "We have a new bus driver.
　　　　　I'm glad. The other one gave us 'H'."
Teacher: "What?"
Student: "'H' just means a headache."

"Teacher, I just can't wait
'til I get old like you."

"Teacher, will you wiggle my tooth for a while?"

"My dad used to look just like Elvis
but he's just older now."

"My aunt has nine bowls of beads.
I guess you realize she is rich, rich, rich."

Teacher, Teacher! Did you know...

"We're not going to Grandma's for Christmas
'cause my brother says Santa won't be there."

Jo Anne Spiceland

"Did you know that if your
favorite number is nine
that means you won't ever
have to have kids?"

"My mom put me in bed for two days last night."

"My cat is pregnant
and my dog is in heat. Wow!"

"Teacher, do you just take
our snack money so you can get rich?"

"I know how to play Tee Ball
but I just can't hit the ball."

"My sister thinks her hair
is the most important thing in the world."

At Housekeeping Center:
    "You can't ding-a-ling anymore!
I've already said Goodbye!"

"I think I'm becoming a man—
I found a hair on my toe last night."

"I have a sore on my leg
and I wish it would quit soring!"

Teacher, Teacher! Did you know...

"My daddy had three hairs on his chest
when he married my mom."

"My grandmama gave me
a couple of million dollars
and I'm going to buy me a new watch."

"I can go bare footed
'cause I'm hard footed."

"Teacher, I'm left-handed but that's just the way life goes."

"Teacher, do you want to buy our house?
We're going to try to sell it 'cause the
electric bill is thirty thousand dollars a month."

"My brother got a medal
for graduating from high school."

"I want my tooth out
but I'm just too 'chicken' to pull it out."

Near Easter:
"Don't dare call me tonight
'cause I'll be boiling eggs tonight."

Jo Anne Spiceland

"My granddaddy died last week.
He was twenty-eight years old."

"Teacher, do you know
where my dad used to be?
In the Boy Scouts."

At the Housekeeping Center:
"But I have to call you 'honey.'
That's what my dad calls my mother."

"I don't want to play married.
Let's just play live together."

"I've got some grown-up teeth in my mouth."

"Teacher, do you mean we can use any of the
things at the Art Center?"
"Yes."
"Well, you're nicer than you usually are!"

Student 1: "Did you get a new sweater for Christmas!"
Student 2: "Yes, but clothes were things that certainly
weren't on my list."

"I'm building something that is very incredible!"

"We have some next door kitties."

Teacher, Teacher! Did you know...

"I'm sorry I whistle so much
but sometimes my whistle
just has to come out."

On October:
"Teacher, it's Pumpkin Time!"

"Teacher, is kicking a car against the law?"

"I stayed up 'til early last night."

"Will we have a fire drill some day?"

Teacher: "And what does Smokey the Bear tell us to do?"
Student: "Smoke!"

"Oh, my legs are getting dizzy."

"My brother has lost eighty-eight teeth."

"Teacher, and how did you get to be
kind of like a Kindergarten teacher?"

"We went fishing last night
and we used pimientos."

Jo Anne Spiceland

"There's a girl in my neighborhood that I don't like
and I'm trying to fix a trap to catch her."

                    "At church yesterday,
                    I turned the preacher out
                    and played Tic Tac Toe."

"I think my dad does something
in the bedroom
but he won't tell me what."

                    "I think my mama's friend is
                    going to get her baby took out today."

"When I went to St. Louis,
I was so excited, I went to the bathroom!"

                    "We have tiger traps set in our yard
                    but we haven't caught any yet."

"Oh! My head! I forgot to bring my brains!"

                    "My dog gets hot spots.
                    She chews and chews
                    'til she gets those hot spots."

"I just have a plain grandmother—
she don't have no husband."

Teacher, Teacher! Did you know...

"What's going on today?
I don't have any products to work on."

"Teacher, did you know
a comet hit my friend's house last night?"

"Teacher, today I feel just like a little shrimp."

Jo Anne Spiceland

Teacher: "Do you have a cold today?"
Student: "No, I just had a heart attack."

"These boys are driving me crazy!
I guess it's 'cause I have this bun in my hair."

"This puzzle looks so delicious
I just can't quit putting it together."

"You may not believe this but
I have a girl friend and she can already write her name."

"Teacher, I'm going on a
honeymoon with my mom."

"Teacher, will you make some
tracks on my paper so I can write my name?"

"Teacher, I don't know for sure
but I believe that silly boy is gay."

Student 1: "I saw lots of pretty
Easter baskets at Sears yesterday."
Student 2: "You mean the Easter Bunny has to go
to Sears to get all that stuff?"

"When all the people in the world die, Teacher,
will they still show cartoons on TV?"

Teacher, Teacher! Did you know...

"It's my dad's birthday
and I don't know how old he is
but we couldn't get all the candles
on his cake."

"Teacher, what's the biggest number in the whole world?"
"I really don't know."
"You mean you're a teacher and you don't know?"

While pushing the merry-go-round: "Come on, Women, let's show the men our stuff!"

"I wasn't absent yesterday—
I was just out of town."

"Teacher, I got you a
hundred-dollar ring for Christmas,
but my mama kept it."

"Know why they call me 'Flash'?
Because I finish my papers so fast."

Jo Anne Spiceland

"I forgot how to write my name
but it just flied back in my head."

"Teacher, if you won't be my friend,
I'll get the principal to spank you."

At Listening Center when the record was over:
"Teacher, this record just lost its words."

"Mommy gave me cough syrup
and I only coughed once."

"If you are 'hyper'
doesn't that mean you are crazy?"

"You may not know we are sisters
but in God's eyes we are."

"I'm never going to pull my mittens off.
They're too hard to get on.
I'll just wear them forever."

"Teacher, ain't raisins just grapes that died?"

"If I don't get what I want at home,
I just stamp my feet—then I do."

Teacher, Teacher! Did you know...

"Teacher, do like to lick catsup as much as I do?"

>"I believe in Jesus
>and Care Bears
>and that's all."

"My daddy had a belly
and a stone in it last night
and he had to go to the hospital."

>"My dad was born the same time I was."

>"Teacher, did you know
>that girls can marry girls
>and boys can marry boys?"

Student 1: "I know you have to be a girl to
          be a Christian."
Student 2: "No you don't. My daddy is a
          Christian but my mama is a waitress."

>"Today is my daddy's birthday—
>he isn't old—he's just fifteen and a half."

Teacher: "Where do peanuts come from?"
Student: "From a peanut butter tree."

Student, trying to find a page in a book:
    "Teacher, what channel do we have to turn to?"

Jo Anne Spiceland

"You'll get chicken pox
    if you chase chickens."

Teacher, Teacher! Did you know...

"Look at that rabbit!
It looks just like a Playboy Bunny!"

"My sister is little—my mom just borned her."

"I want to stay in Kindergarten forever.
But, then, I'd have to be a midget, wouldn't I?"

"My dog is half brown and half collie."

"Teacher, don't you have to pay to go to weddings?
I think it just costs one dollar."

"Teacher, I have a question
about <u>that</u> question."

"Whew!
This room is getting
too stuffed with kids."

"When the election was off the other night
we had to eat bologna sandwiches."

"If you hurry when you
are coloring or doing your work,
that means you are just a pig."

Jo Anne Spiceland

"Look at this, Teacher.
This kind of writing is called Volcano scribbling."

"Grandma calls my Grandpa a bone head!"

"I play games with Mama on the floor—
then she can't get back up!"

"Grandpa always says 'Howdy Dooty' when he sees me and wants me to kiss him."

"My mom got married
and she had to go to a hotel."

"I got to watch a 'R' rated movie last night!"

"My dad has a naked tooth brush."

"My mama used check money."

"Teacher, you forgot
to give me a gift certificate
for counting to 100."

Teacher, Teacher! Did you know...

"I snored so much that my tooth came out!"

"My mom is going to have a baby in about three years."

"I can spell my name just up in the air."

"Me and my mother is twins."

"I don't think I can write today—
I had to shake hands too much at church, yesterday."

"My mother doesn't like taking care of us kids."

"My mom got her hair whited yesterday."

"Teacher, I can't learn that.
My brain just isn't very big."

"When my mother prays,
she always ends with 'all-men.'
I don't know what she means."

Jo Anne Spiceland

Student 1: "Do you think my teacher will like my picture?"
Student 2: "Oh, yes, she likes everybody's."

Teacher, Teacher! Did you know...

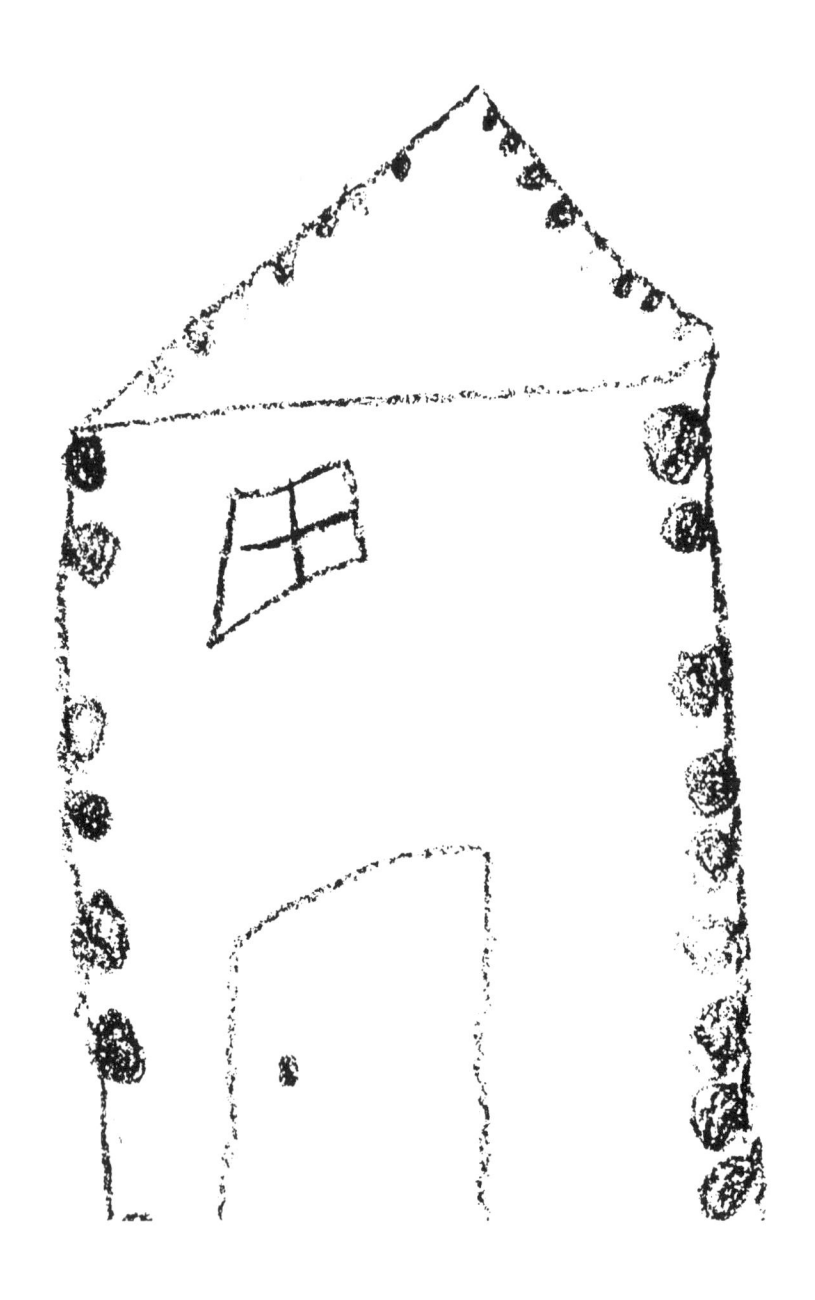

"We're getting a new house and two thousand dogs."

Jo Anne Spiceland

"I need some new brakes in my feet."

"Teacher, is this a boy's purse?"

"Teacher, when you get to be thirty-eight,
that's as long as you will live."

At snack time:
"Teacher, tell them to eat their carrots.
They're good for your blood."

"Do we have a Katy Day off?"
(K.E.A.—Kentucky Education Association)

"He's acting silly—
I think he needs brain surgery.
Teacher, could you do it?"

"We took my mom to the hospital
in the funeral ambulance."

"Cookies are the best snacks we have except cakes."

Teacher, Teacher! Did you know...

"I can't come to school tomorrow
if my dog is sick."

"This is a good snack and it's <u>contritious</u>."
(nutritious)

"I couldn't come to school yesterday
'cause I had a stomach."

"Our neighbors got <u>translated</u>
to another state."
(transferred)

"I have two friends that can speak English."

"Can I have a birth certificate
for my tooth I lost yesterday?"

"I don't aim to ever get married
but I may just have to get a man."

"I can tell a difference between boys and girls by looking
at their faces."

Jo Anne Spiceland

"I'll never date when I grow up.
I'll just go to college."

"I brought you an apple today.
It didn't grow on a tree, it just grew underground."

"Teacher, I have some terrible news—
I can't come to school Friday."

Getting children into the cars:
Teacher: "Oh, look at that cute dog in your car!"
Student: "That ain't a dog! It's my aunt!"

"Teacher, will you pray for my big brother?
He really needs help."

"Teacher, from living here in Kentucky
where I live, it's only twenty miles to Florida."

Teacher, Teacher! Did you know...

"Teacher, If you'll
take me home with you,
I'll do your dishes."

"Is George Washington
the <u>farter</u> of our country?"
(father)

"George Washington was an
apple tree before he was president."

"George's name was Martha
before he was president."

"For Thanksgiving,
I'd like to eat turkey, rabbits,
fish, carrots and pumpkin pie."

"If you marry your sister,
will you have to go to jail?"

"I have a halfway cousin that lives close to me."

"Teacher, I just can't do my work
'cause it makes my hands hot."

Jo Anne Spiceland

"My mother put me in bed
for two days last night."

"We saw bears at the pizza place last night
and nobody <u>alternated</u> them."

"When I grow up,
I want to be a football player,
a baseball player, and a car fixer."

Student 1: "I'm going to Six Flags this summer."
Student 2: "I'm going to Seven Flags!"

Teacher, Teacher! Did you know...

"When I get to be 35,
I'm going scuba diving for treasures."

"I just can't wait to get old!"

"We watched a good program yesterday night."

Teacher:
"What country do we live in?"
Student:
"Kentucky—I know 'cause I saw the Wildcats play!"

"I'm giving my girlfriend a ring
and we're going to date."

"My brother eats so messy
he resembles a hog."

"My grandpaw always wears a pink shirt
but most of the time my grandmaw wears pajamas."

Jo Anne Spiceland

"My granddaddy calls me a 'goo goo' girl."

"My mother got married last night
but they wouldn't let me go on a trip with them."

"When my mom washes her teeth,
she has to take them out."

"My mother wears
the funniest underwear
I've ever seen!"

"Isn't there such a thing as a six dollar bill?"

"My mom is in love with a movie star
but she's still married to my dad."

"We don't give Mom anything
for her birthday except a cake."

"Last night, I counted to a million and nine to my parents."

Teacher, Teacher! Did you know...

"My dad is 21 years old
    and my mom is 14."

    "Look! Teacher! It's thirty o'clock!"

"My mom is a forgetter.
She can't remember anything!"

    "When I was born,
    I hatched from an egg."

Student to student:
    "Get that fat off your face! It looks horrible."

    "We discovered some of our
    Christmas presents
    but Mom doesn't know it yet."

    "Teacher, why do you give us
    such mischievous tests?"

    "Teacher, my earache hurts!"

Jo Anne Spiceland

"If I tell a story, do I have to tell the truth?"

Note to teacher:
   "Teacher, I lack you vere much."

Teacher, Teacher! Did you know...

"Teacher, I wish you was my mother."

"My mom knows all the boys
are just crazy about me."

"Teacher, did you know
some of our clothes is made from sheep's cotton?"

Teacher: "Why did we have to set our clocks back last
            night?"
Student: "Because we got more work to do."

"Teacher, we won't start
being Indian blooded
'til we get 18 years old."

"My mom made Dad
sleep on the couch last night."

"When I go outside and play,
   Mom always makes me take a bath."

"Teacher! Teacher! Look at him! He's my lover boy!"

Jo Anne Spiceland

"I can't run on my ankle.
If I do I may have to get an <u>exeration</u>."
(operation)

"My mom's going to be rich.
I'm buying her a plate that costs $2.50."

"My puppy had doggies a week ago."

"Next year, I'll play baseball
but you have to be real old
before you can play."

"Teacher, won't the devil get you if you tell a lie?"

Student 1: "Jesus is really God."
Student 2: "No He isn't! He's God's son."

"Teacher, my mama can't have
any more babies so would you
have one and give it to me?"

"I drove our car out of the garage
last night and into the yard—
but Daddy came out and spanked me."

Teacher, Teacher! Did you know...

> "My mom lets me watch
> R-rated movies sometimes
> but I'm not supposed to tell you."

Boy to girl: "Do you have a boyfriend?"
Girl: "No."
Boy: "Will you be mine, then?"

> "My boyfriend and I broke up.
> I just think he's stupid."

> "I can tell my teachers apart
> 'cause one wears glasses and one don't."

"We go to the Higgly Piggly's to the grocery."

> "I fell at recess and hurt my brain."

Jo Anne Spiceland

"Do you know why Rudolph's nose is red?
He bumped it!"

Teacher, Teacher! Did you know...

"My dad has to work—
even on Halloween!"

Jo Anne Spiceland

Kids and words—they all go together! Listening to their vocabulary sometimes excites you and makes a teacher have a fun day.

"Teacher, do you remember the <u>Revelation</u> War?"

    A child started writing a story like this:
        "Once a pony time. . . ."
    (Makes sense if you think of it!)

"We're having a new <u>rooth</u> put on our house." (roof)

    "We went to a cave
    and found some <u>flagtites</u>."
    (stalagtites)

Teacher, Teacher! Did you know...

"In <u>Freeschool</u>, we took a long trip to the lake."
(Preschool)

"Teacher, I believe he has the <u>Debble</u> in him."
(Devil)

"I lost my card and my money
that I brought for the <u>crooked</u> children."
(crippled)

"Did you know I sleep in
a <u>bump</u> bed every night?"
(bunk)

"Teacher, I was a ring <u>barrier</u>
at a wedding last night."
(bearer)

"It's raining! I need an <u>underbrella</u>."
(umbrella)

"Here comes Smokey and the <u>Band Aids</u>."
(Bandit)

"Teacher, they are <u>unbeying</u> your rules today."
(obeying)

Jo Anne Spiceland

"I know a word that begins with 'F'—
<u>Feteran's</u> Day!"
(Veteran's)

"Last night my mom gave me a <u>laxident</u>."
(laxative)

"Let's poop a while. I'm tired."

"Amos can't talk.
I guess he has <u>magnesia</u>." (amnesia)
(Amos was our elephant.)

"Do we have to <u>return</u> our papers today?"

"Teacher, I really like to play <u>opoly</u>!"
(Monopoly)

"My mother put a <u>assahol</u> in my ear last night."
(alcohol)

"When we went to Florida,
we went to the <u>Apricot</u> Center."
(Epcot)

"I want to be a <u>vallerina</u> when I get big."
(ballerina)

101

Teacher, Teacher! Did you know...

"My mom rid her bike
all the way up on our roof."
(rode)

"My mom's friend got a divorcement yesterday."
(divorce)

"We went to the Umpire Farm last year."
(Empire)

"I saw a chopperhead snake last night."
(copperhead)

"We had cob-on-corn last night for dinner."
(corn-on-the-cob)

"We rode an idabator up to
the eighth floor at the store last night."
(elevator)

"We ate at Mr. Spaghetti's last night
and it was really good."
(Mr. Gatti's)

"We are getting a new porch—
a screamed in one."
(screened)

Jo Anne Spiceland

"I'm so hot I think I'm <u>aspiring</u>."
(perspiring)

"I got a new <u>T. V.</u> shot today."
(T. B.)

"Teacher, you haven't <u>weight lifted</u> me yet." (weighed)

"When will we all make something
out of <u>instruction</u> paper?"
(construction)

"My daddy acts like a <u>aprechaun</u>
and gives us lots of candy."
(leprechaun)

"A girl in the sixth grade <u>misbehaviored</u>
and had to miss recess for six weeks."
(misbehaved)

"My dog has <u>poisonous</u> all over him."
(poison)

"I can always <u>reap</u> my mother's mind."
(read)

Teacher, Teacher! Did you know...

"My cute little cat just <u>slips</u> up its milk."
(sips)

"Teacher, is this the day we get our <u>credit cards</u>?"
(report cards)

"We saw a movie last night about the <u>Burst</u> of Jesus."
(Birth)

"We go swimming in the summer at the <u>Comic</u> Motel."
(Comet)

"My daddy likes to eat <u>horse relishes</u>."
(horseradishes)

"Teacher, I get <u>'fused</u> on these things."

"Teacher, lets sing <u>Silence at Night</u>."
(*Silent Night*)

"We are watching on T.V. <u>'Our Kingdom Chum'</u>."
(Our Kingdom Come)

Jo Anne Spiceland

"I wasn't here yesterday 'cause I had an <u>energy</u>."
(allergy)

"I had to go to the hospital today
to get a blood <u>vessel</u> test."

"My favorite pudding is <u>hopscotch</u> pudding."
(butterscotch)

"My sister is having <u>containers</u> put on her teeth."
(retainers)

"My mom bought <u>worms</u>
to curl her hair with."

"I got some new shoes
at the shoe <u>repartment</u>."
(department)

"We have a new <u>creature</u> at our church."
(preacher)

"I go to the <u>Three Wheel</u> Baptist Church."
(Free Will)

Teacher, Teacher! Did you know...

"Why does Daddy put that
 banana freeze in our car?"
(anti-freeze)

Student, standing in line waiting
for a photograph to be made:
"I sure am glad I have my underroos on!"

"I'm getting a new Simonese cat for Christmas."
(Siamese)

"We have a new diagonal clock at home."
(digital)

"I was awake all Christmas night.
I had congestors."
(congestion)

"I'm going to be a batographer when I grow up."
(photographer)

"We always put foxcide on my cuts."
(peroxide)

Jo Anne Spiceland

"Teacher, did you know
a volcano <u>interrupted</u> yesterday?"
(erupted)

"Teacher, do you remember
when we saw that <u>prayer bug</u> on our window?"
(praying mantis)

"Do you like my new <u>Hobby Hobby</u> skirt?"
(Holly Hobby)

"We came to the <u>Free T. O.</u> last night."
(P. T. O.)

"Teacher, do you know a song
called <u>The Old Ragged Cross</u>?"
(*The Old Rugged Cross*)

Student, while singing *My Country 'Tis of Thee*:
"land of the <u>villian's</u> pride."
(Pilgrims)

"My brother is sick—
he has the <u>weasles</u>."
(measles)

"She's not here,
she's <u>accident</u>."
(absent)

107

Teacher, Teacher! Did you know...

"Mom went to a <u>Tufferware</u> party last night."
(Tupperware)

"I'm getting a <u>fool</u> table for Christmas."
(pool)

"Teacher, do you wear panty <u>toes</u> to school?"
(hose)

"Can we ride the <u>America-go-round</u> today?"
(merry-go-round)

"Teacher, I can't think!
I've lost my <u>concentrate</u>."
(concentration)

"Teacher, he borrowed by glue without <u>commission</u>!"
(permission)

Singing *America the Beautiful*:
"and brown us good through brotherhood"
(crown thy good. . . .)

"My favorite TV program is *Lagney and Casey*."
(Cagney and Lacey)

Jo Anne Spiceland

"We got a new <u>Ham</u> dog last night—
you know, the one whose ears touch the floor."
(hound)

"At Brownies yesterday, we made <u>puffets</u>."
(puppets)

Teacher, Teacher! Did you know...

"Teacher, can I tell you how to cut a turkey?
Shoot it, then clean it, and cook it ten minutes."

Jo Anne Spiceland

"Teacher, I love you.
Why do you sit there doing nothing?"

Jo Anne Spiceland

Letters from sixth-grade students

Dear Mrs. Spiceland:

It's been a long time since Kindergarten, but I still remember someone sitting in your rocking chair and reading a book to the rest of the kids. I remember that as being my favorite part of the day. I also remember the song we had for learning the days of the week. I loved Center Time, too. (Especially the Reading Center.)

Thank you for teaching me and for making Kindergarten so enjoyable. I love you and will never forget you!

*Love always,
(A sixth-grade student)*

Teacher, Teacher! Did you know...

Dear Mrs. Spiceland:

I enjoyed Kindergarten. It was probably my favorite year along with one of my favorite teachers. You were nice to all of us and gave us all a lot of attention. I learned a lot for a Kindergarten kid that year and I had lots of fun. I'm in the sixth grade shoving off to Middle School. Maybe I'll come to visit you if I find the time between sports, band and school work.

Your friend,
(A sixth-grade student)

Jo Anne Spiceland

Dear Mrs. Spiceland:

How are you doing? I hope you remember me. Well, you probably will. I was always a big pest. I thought I might write to my favorite teacher because I didn't have many friends in Kindergarten but you were really my best friend and you still are. That is why you are my favorite teacher.

Your pest,
(A sixth-grade student)

Teacher, Teacher! Did you know...

Jo Anne Spiceland

Favorite Quotes
I want to remember...

Teacher, Teacher! Did you know...

Jo Anne Spiceland

Teacher, Teacher! Did you know...

Jo Anne Spiceland

Jo Anne Spiceland

Teacher, Teacher! Did you know. . . .

Mail to:
Jo Anne Spiceland
7206 Benton Road
Paducah, KY 42003

Please send me _____ copies of

Teacher, Teacher!
    Did you know. . . . @ $ 12.95 each   _____

Postage & handling   3.50

Kentucky residents add 6% sales tax @   .78 each   _____

Total enclosed   _____

Make check payable to Jo Anne Spiceland

Ship to:
NAME
_____

ADDRESS
_____

CITY _____ STATE _____ ZIP _____

Please Copy

Jo Anne Spiceland

Teacher, Teacher! Did you know. . . .

Mail to:
Jo Anne Spiceland
7206 Benton Road
Paducah, KY 42003

Please send me _____ copies of

*Teacher, Teacher!
     Did you know. . . .* @ $ 12.95 each   _____

Postage & handling   ___3.50___

Kentucky residents add 6% sales tax @   .78 each   _____

Total enclosed   _____

Make check payable to Jo Anne Spiceland

Ship to:
NAME
_____

ADDRESS
_____

CITY _____ STATE _____ ZIP _____

Please Copy